T0276647

PhotoArk

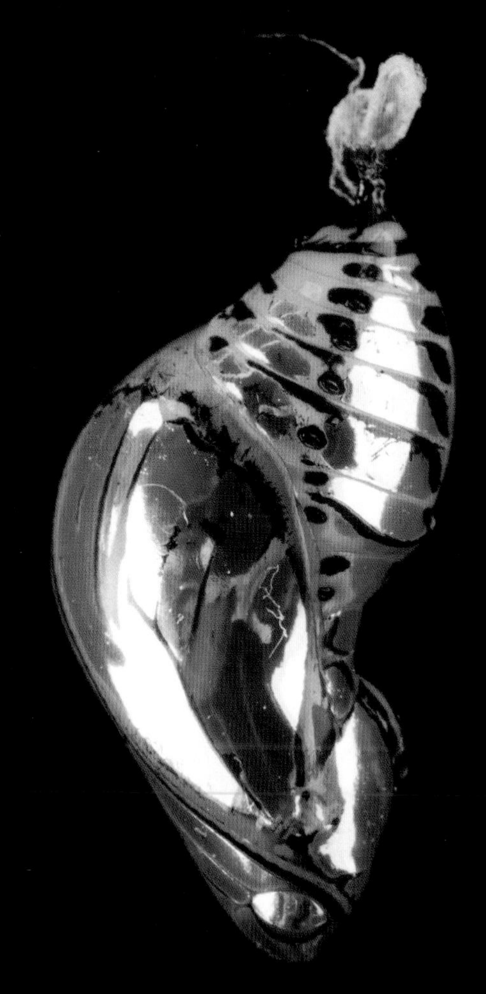

Celebrating our **WILD WORLD** in **poetry** and **pictures**

NATIONAL GEOGRAPHIC
PHOTO ARK
JOEL SARTORE

Photographs by **JOEL SARTORE,** Photo Ark Creator

Words by **KWAME ALEXANDER,** Winner of the Newbery Medal

With Mary Rand Hess and Deanna Nikaido

NATIONAL GEOGRAPHIC
Washington, D.C.

chorus of **creatures**

singing our names

see what we can save—**together**

look into these **eyes**

full of **secret**

places to **hide**

and

play

a feathered **rainbow dance** . . .

. . . . . curiosity that LEAPS

homes of courage

on **humble backs**

this is **not a race**

embracing **wonder**

SLIDING and GLIDING

waiting for you to notice

spots blend unseen

so they can **STALK**, swim

sneak up on us

listen to the rumble

giant stomping feet

calling brothers ... sisters

blink and you'll miss

the hush of waves, **tiny feet**

scurrying inside dunes

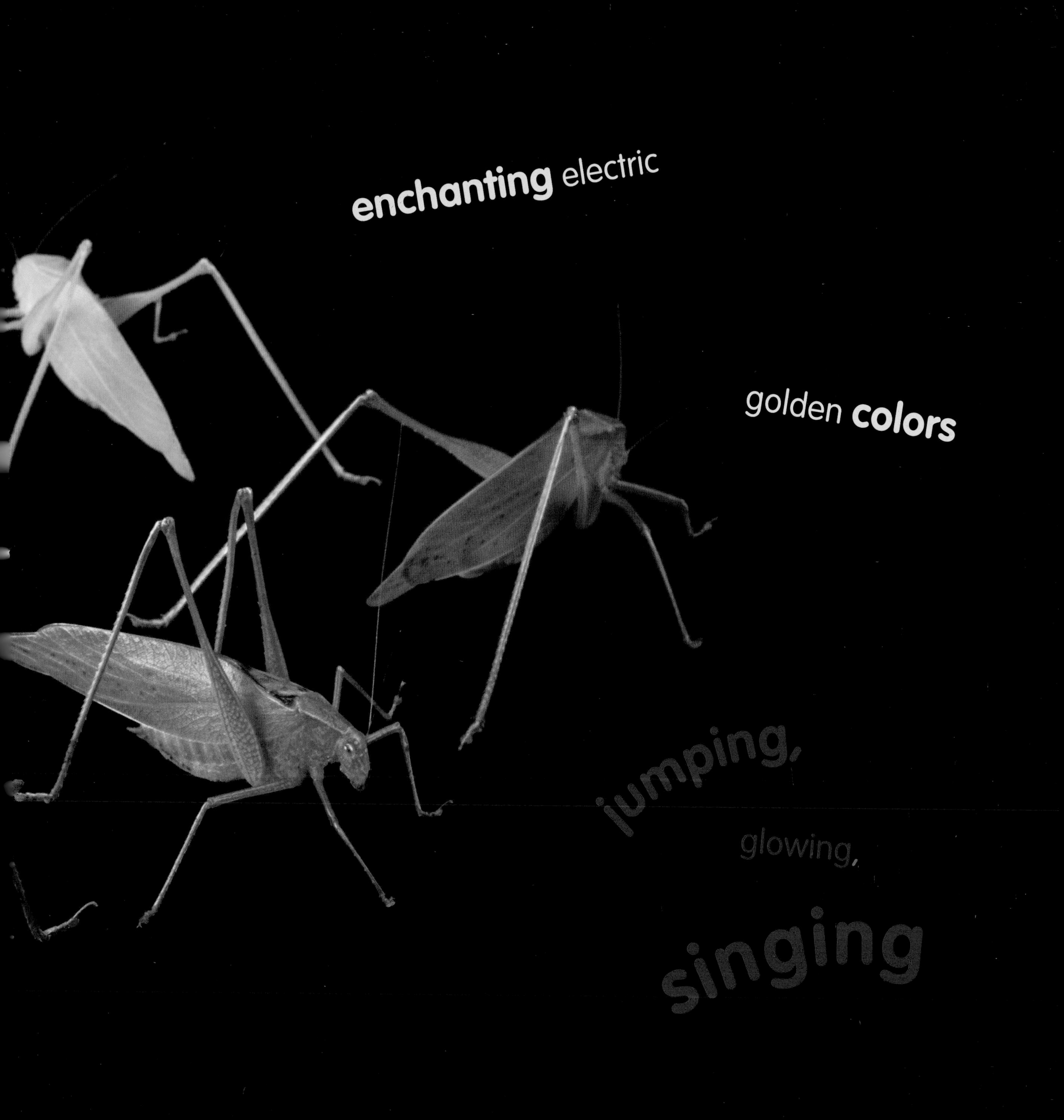

enchanting electric

golden **colors**

jumping,

glowing,

singing

wings like a **cape,**

ready for **flight**

into the sweet, **dark night**

WILD at heart

with slow, measured moves

and eyes **BIG** as **two sunsets**

how many **feathers** . . . does it take to make a **wing**

TO FLY, SHARE SKY

coils of hiss

Mohawk **plume** . . . . . . sharp, stinging **beauty**

from **glistening sea**

to **rising sun**

color me **ANCIENT** and **SACRED**

turquoise and gold

camouflage in the trees

moods changing with the breeze

HOWL
like you mean it . . . the world is listening

a pair of **claws**

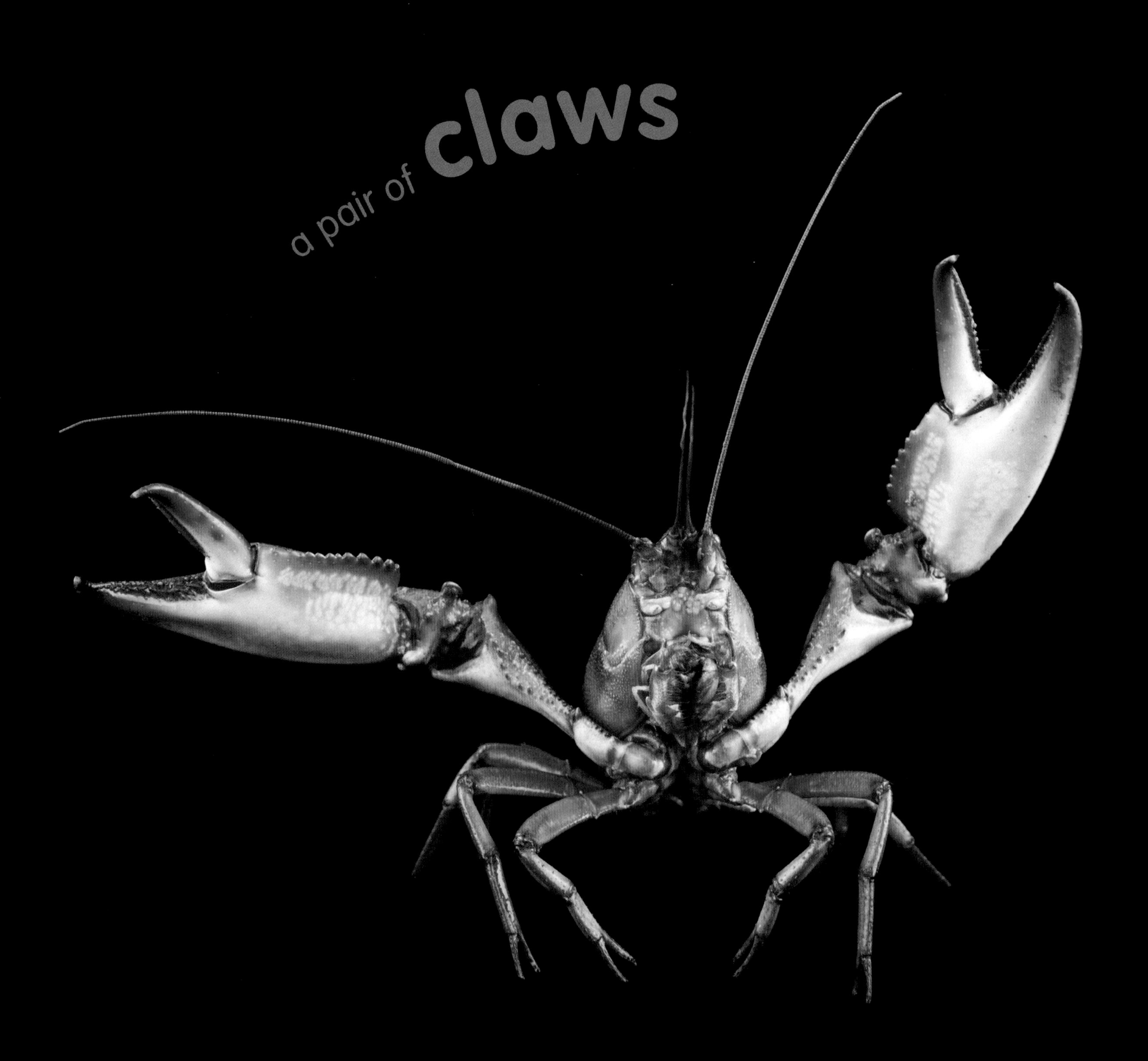

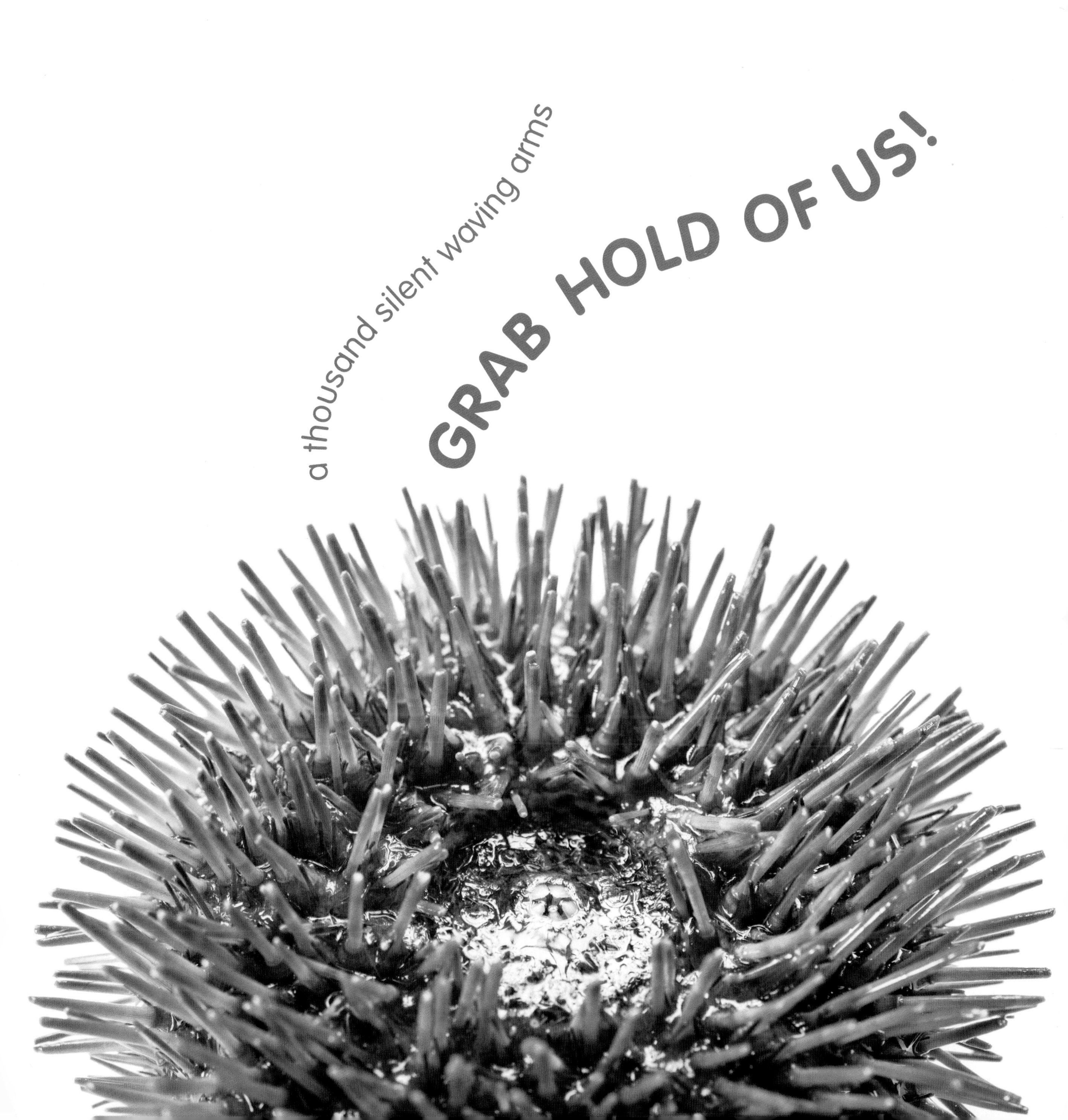
a thousand silent waving arms
GRAB HOLD OF US!

innocent wander

tiny growls

new to the **chase**

a **hundred feet**

walking without a sound

one direction

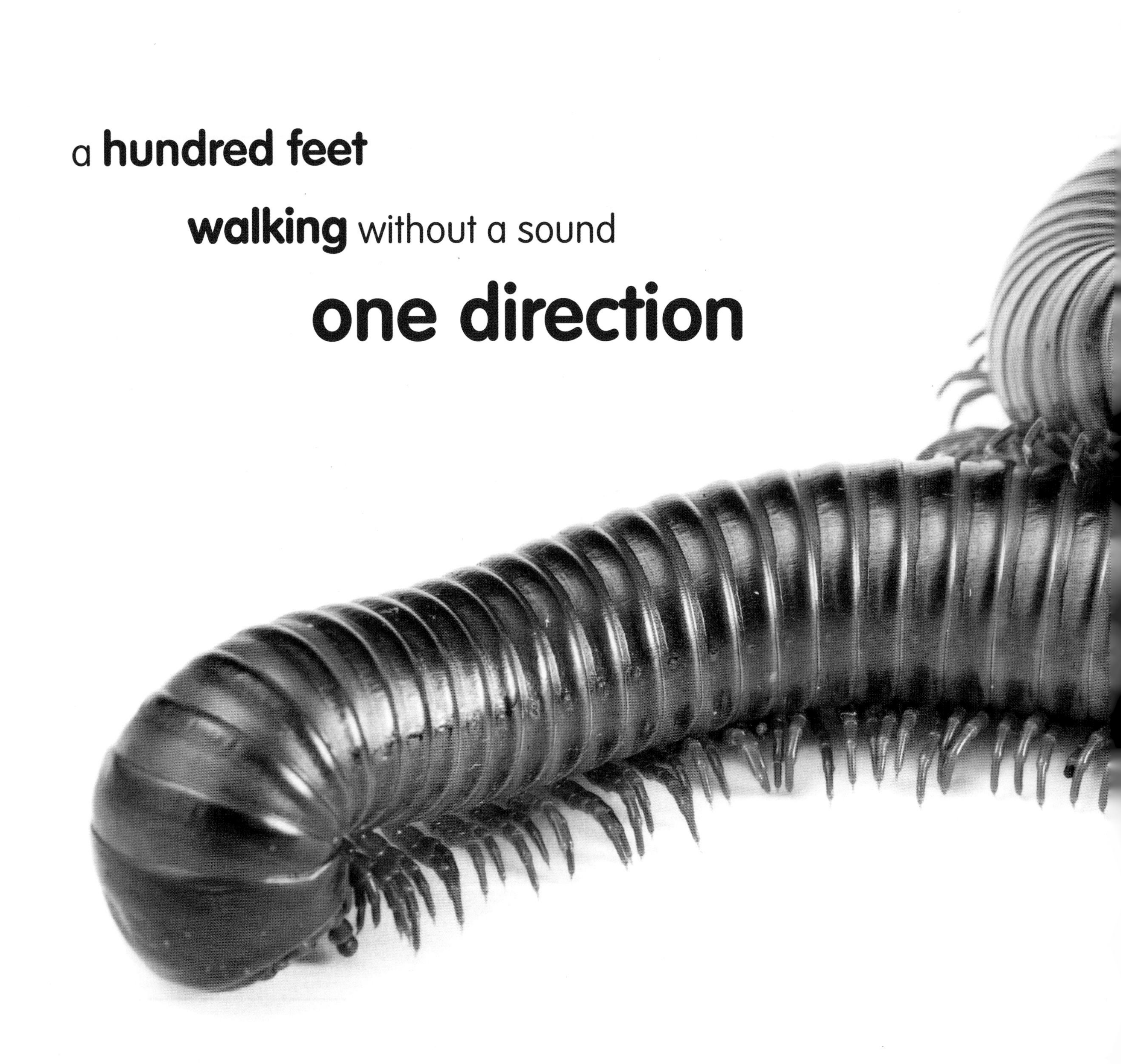

spooky webs spinning

a **deadly** tattoo:

STAY AWAY!

strong, yet **gentle . . . black** and **white**

championing human nature

grandfather of the **hunt**

FIERCE and **FAST**

and **favored,** forever?

A Note From the Photographer

At its heart, the Photo Ark was born out of necessity.

I have been sent around the world by *National Geographic* magazine for more than 20 years to take photographs of people, places, and animals. There have been assignments to capture images of the fiercest predators, the shyest sea creatures, the most beautiful birds, and so many more. Several years ago, I started to see that people weren't paying much attention to the fate of all the other species we share this planet with. Without action, and soon, I worried that many animals could go extinct.

The Photo Ark is my answer to this. By introducing the entire world to thousands of photographs of mammals, birds, reptiles, amphibians, fish, and even insects, I hope we can get everyone following, liking, texting, tweeting, and even talking about this wondrous world of ours.

In the Photo Ark, every creature is equal. I use simple black and white backgrounds, which make all animals appear to be the same size, no matter how large or small they might be in the wild. Each photo also shows you the amazing detail of a creature's scales, skin, or feathers; their eyes, antennae, or legs—each creature with its own kind of stunning beauty. A slippery minnow in the Photo Ark appears as big as a shark, and a tiny tiger beetle as impressive as a mighty tiger.

I want people around the world to look these animals in the eye, and then fall in love with creatures as dazzling as a pheasant or as odd as an octopus. And once we love something, won't we do anything to save it?

So just how can you get started saving species? There are many ways—and it starts by protecting our planet. Defend animal ecosystems by reducing, reusing, and recycling every product you can. Think sustainably, knowing that whatever you buy is made somewhere and out of something. Ask yourself: Is it good for the planet? And talk to your family about becoming a member of your local zoo or aquarium. They're the real arks now, working hard every day to save everything from aardvarks to zebras.

I believe all of us have a great capacity to care. And when we do, we can accomplish amazing things. I've seen it with my own eyes many times: The wildlife rehabilitator who opens her home to treat injured small mammals; the private breeder who works for years to save critically endangered birds; or the teacher who shares his love of butterflies with generations of children.

All are environmental heroes to me. You can be one too, if you just look around, and care.

Now, what will you do to make this world a better place?

—Joel Sartore

The National Geographic Photo Ark is a multiyear effort with photographer Joel Sartore to photograph every captive species to inspire people to save those most vulnerable, while also funding conservation projects focused on those in most critical need of protection.

A Note From the Writer

Lately I have been drawn to collaborative projects. Part of it is I seem to have more ideas these days, and less time to implement them alone. But, also, I love the tremendous feeling of being connected to like-minded artists who inspire me. Who encourage me to become better. As a poet. As a man. As a human being. It is that same feeling of connectedness and humanity that brought me and my dear writerly friends, Deanna and Mary, to *Photo Ark* and the incredible artistic preservation of Joel Sartore.

Speaking of poetry, this project resonated with me as a writer because of the parallel nature between powerful photographs and poetry as narrative—which is in its own way a kind of literary snapshot. Both have the ability to bypass the skin and enter through the heart, transforming what is often difficult to convey into something universal.

I wondered how to approach the subject matter of endangered animals with children like my own eight-year-old daughter, who has many questions, and who is more aware of things than I sometimes give her credit for. How would I bring forth a visual conversation, full of rhythm and imagery and movement and conciseness that plants seeds so she knows they need watering? Even more, how would my page live up to the majestic and magical stage that Joel has presented to us so lovely?

After working with hundreds of students of all ages, I have found when using the Japanese form of haiku that something about its brevity creates an instant connection. The more sparse and condensed the language is, the more potent the message. Joel Sartore's photographs are exquisite visual haiku that capture something even words cannot, and yet the combination of the two creates a landscape, a third language only the heart knows. Thirty-two of these precious animals are given special attention in this book, but there are thousands more. My hope, and Mary's prayer, and Deanna's belief is that this is only the beginning of the many ways in which we can address this home we all share, whether human or animal. Change can begin with a thought; a conversation; a photograph; a poem.

—Kwame Alexander

Haiku

Traditional Japanese haiku is a seventeen-syllable, three-line poem—where the first line has five syllables, the second line has seven, and the third has five. Known for its concentrated brevity and reference to nature, it can sometimes vary in syllables and theme due to cultural and untranslatable differences in language (consider the word "haiku" itself has two syllables in English and three in Japanese). In any language, the beauty of this poetry form is in its concise power, and its ability to frame in some abstract way a complete thought with the subtle qualities of a question. It's the perfect complement to these incredible photographs. Both should inspire continued conversation. Look at the images in *Photo Ark* and try creating your own haiku!